I0154520

Praise for Is it Just?

Is it Just? is not only a very helpful tool to assist in studying the book of Jeremiah, but also a very helpful tool to assist you in learning the heart of God for justice. In a world that cries out for justice, *Is it Just?* will ground you in a biblical view of what is just and how you can be an agent of justice in your life. I wholeheartedly recommend this excellent resource from Trevor Whitman.

—**Bo Noonan**, Lead Elder, New Community Church Tacoma

***

This book is a powerful and timely exploration of the themes found in the book of Jeremiah—idolatry, self-sufficiency, and the relentless faithfulness of God. With clarity and depth, Trevor brings ancient truths into sharp focus for today's world. It's a stirring call to examine our hearts, trust God's promises, and remain faithful in times of uncertainty. A must-read for anyone seeking to hear God's voice in challenging seasons.

—**Aaron Gentile,** Family Life Pastor, Life Center Tacoma

***

Trevor has written a fresh thematic walk through of the book of Jeremiah. It's perfect for a group seeking to go deeper into an often overlooked and misunderstood book. It's also helpful for someone seeking to navigate personal renewal or deeper formation. His thoughtful approach will allow the reader to reimagine Jeremiah in a personal way so that the prophet will lead you deeper into the character of God. Grateful for this work!

—**Brian Wilson,** Dean of Students, Cascade Christian Schools

***

Trevor takes crucial lessons from the book of Jeremiah and expands it to not only a holistic understanding of the biblical narrative but also gives specific and challenging personal application through each theme for us as followers of Jesus. Incredible stuff!

—**Tristan Norris,** Young Adults Pastor, Crossroads Community Church

***

What does God's justice truly look like—and how are we called to embody it? In *Is it Just?*, Trevor guides readers through the book of Jeremiah with clarity, conviction, and thoughtful questions that draw us into deeper reflection. He helps us see justice not merely as a cultural or social concern, but as a direct expression of God's character. I highly recommend this engaging study of Jeremiah.

—**Rachel Snodgrass,** Child & Family Therapist, Puyallup Tribal Health Authority

***

Trevor does an outstanding job of taking the timeless themes found in the prophet Jeremiah's warnings to Israel and connecting them to our present-day walk as followers of Jesus. He skillfully draws parallels between the Old Testament context and the New Testament era we live in, helping us see that the spiritual struggles of ancient times—issues like justice, self-sufficiency, idolatry, and unrepentant hearts—are still deeply relevant in 2025. As a fellow baseball guy, I especially appreciate Trevor's thoughtful structure—like a good practice plan, his approach is purposeful and intentional. The discussion guide at the end of each chapter is a valuable tool for reflection and application, helping readers digest and engage with the weighty truths drawn from Jeremiah. This

book is a powerful and timely resource for any believer seeking to grow in their faith and remain spiritually grounded and culturally relevant in today's world."
—**Tim Kuykendal,** Director of Athletics, Vertical Sports Maui

***

With clarity and conviction, Trevor shows us that every hardship is an invitation back to God. You'll find yourself in the story, challenged to trust God more deeply in every part of your life.
—**Abi Sovereign**, Youth Director, New Community Church Tacoma

Is it just?

A Thematic Study of the Book of Jeremiah

Trevor Whitman

Published by KHARIS PUBLISHING, an imprint of
KHARIS MEDIA LLC.
Copyright © 2025 Trevor Whitman
ISBN: 978-1-63746-341-3
ISBN: 1-63746-341-3
Library of Congress Control Number:2025944131
All rights reserved. This book or parts thereof may not be
reproduced in any form, stored in a retrieval system, or
transmitted in any form by any means - electronic,
mechanical, photocopy, recording, or otherwise - without
prior written permission of the publisher, except as provided
by United States of America copyright law.
Unless otherwise noted, all Scripture quotations are taken
from the Christan Standard Bible®, Copyright © 2017 by
Holman Bible Publishers. Used by permission. Christian
Standard Bible® and CSB© are federally registered
trademarks of Holman Bible Publishers.
All KHARIS PUBLISHING products are available at special
quantity discounts for bulk purchase for sales promotions,
premiums, fund-raising, and educational needs. For details,
contact:
Kharis Media LLC
Tel: 1-630-909-3405
support@kharispublishing.com
www.kharispublishing.com

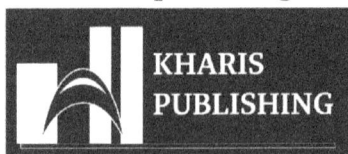

KHARIS
PUBLISHING

Table of Contents

Introduction

The danger in any thematic study of the Bible is the temptation to take verses out of context and apply them prescriptively to your life. Instead of taking specific instructions that were meant for a group of people within a particular time in history, we should glean truths about who God is, what His instructions to others say about Him, and what His expectations are of those who claim to follow Him. Even if we can't take everything literally, we can still observe the Israelites' behavior during that time and apply it to our modern context. We can trust that God is the same yesterday, today, and tomorrow when we read the Scriptures and learn that He reigns eternally and is outside of time.

Many immature believers mistakenly believe that the God of the Old Testament is distinct from the God of the New Testament. The same triune God who created the world, guided the Israelites in the Old Testament, and walked the earth in the New Testament is still here. The Father, Son, and Holy Spirit are all unique persons within the Holy Trinity; they are perfect in unity and live outside the confines of our understanding of time. The reason why some have a hard time wrapping their heads around this is that the teachings of Jesus can seem to stand in stark contrast to the actions of the jealous Father in the Old Testament. However, despite their distinct roles, the entirety of Scripture reveals that they are acting with unity, purpose, and will.

Observing how God speaks to the Israelites in the book of Jeremiah can give a glimpse into what He might say to those who claim to follow Him in the modern Western church. It isn't the same, but in seeing how the Lord deals with their disobedience, unrepentance, and mistreatment of others, it isn't far-fetched to think that this era of believers needs to hear the same message. Some individuals who profess to follow Christ assert that they are solely "eternally focused." And when doing so, they neglect issues that arise in our present day. The issue with that is that God calls us to live in such a manner that we are both now and not yet. We know that there is still a kingdom yet to come (Revelation 21:1), but we also wrestle in the tension that the kingdom is also here. In Luke 17:20-21, Jesus discusses this paradigm: "Once, on being asked by the Pharisees when the kingdom of God would come, Jesus replied, 'The coming of the kingdom of God is not something that can be observed, nor will people say, "Here it is,' or "There it is,' because the kingdom of God is in your midst."

If you live your whole life only waiting for eternity on the other side of death, you are missing what He has called you to do right here, right now. A moment that is not often talked about that demonstrates this reality is when Moses had the opportunity to enter the Promised Land, and the paradigm of eternity that humanity held to that point shifted completely. In Exodus 33, the Israelites had just been found worshiping the golden calf after Moses came down from Mount Sinai. The Lord was rightfully irritated at their lack of faithfulness and patience, so He tells Moses in verses 1-3 to "leave this place, you and the people you brought up out of Egypt, and go up to the land I promised… but I will not go with you…" But Moses understood something that most of us miss. The "Promised Land" isn't heaven, a destination, job, house, family, or any physical thing; it is a relationship with the Lord. He responds in verse 15, "Then Moses said to him, If your presence does not go with us, do not send us up from here." He knew that without God, there is no Promised Land because the relationship with God is the

Promised Land. In the same way, there is a large chunk of people who consider themselves Christians who only want a relationship with God so they can go to heaven. But there is no heaven without God! Heaven is not the promised land; a relationship with Him is. Eternity isn't something we have to wait for; we can start right now. Focusing only on the future makes us miss the people in front of us.

Our lack of empathy as believers toward the world is one of the biggest hindrances to spreading the gospel. Instead of being a light in the darkness, oftentimes, believers are the reason why things are dark to begin with. We often neglect the needs of those around us due to our preoccupation with life after death. Jeremiah expands on this thought at length and links it to a legalistic mindset that focuses on following the traditions and rules of the faith without loving or caring for the people around us.

Jesus addresses this situation in the New Testament in Luke 11:42 when He says, "Woe to you Pharisees, because you give God a tenth of your mint, rue, and all other kinds of garden herbs, but you neglect justice and the love of God. You should have practiced the latter without leaving the former undone." There are many other places where Jesus discusses the legalistic framework that religion can paint us into. When we care more about results, power, wealth, and traditions, it leads people to make allowances for evil because "the ends justify the means."

King Solomon in the book of Proverbs in 16:8 says, "Better a little with righteousness than much gain with injustice." This theme of living righteously, with truth and justice, caring for the vulnerable among us, and faithfully obeying what God has called us to do permeates both the Old and New Testaments, but specifically and most emphatically in the prophets.

In the beginning, God created the heavens and the earth. Adam and Eve sinned, which led to the fall of man and the introduction of sin into the world. Abraham establishes a covenant with God where He will make his descendants as vast as the stars in the sky. Isaac, the son of Abraham, has a son he names Jacob, who God renamed Israel. Jacob had twelve sons who became the tribes of Israel, one of whom was his favorite son, Joseph. Through Joseph's faithfulness, the twelve tribes found refuge in Egypt during the famine that had struck the land. Over time, the Egyptians were worried about how large the tribe of Israel was becoming, so they enslaved them. God freed the Israelites when Moses led them out into the wilderness. That generation never saw the Promised Land of Canaan because of their disobedience and grumbling, but Joshua finished what Moses started by taking them over the Jordan River and receiving the inheritance God promised them. After the conquest of the land was complete, God established judges to help govern the people. God consistently rescues them, but they quickly revert to their old habits. Eventually, the people grumble enough that God finally relents and gives them a physical king, even though He wanted to be theirs all along. Saul is the first king of Israel, followed by David and then Solomon, which led to a conglomeration of wicked and righteous kings. The kings eventually became so wicked and unrepentant that God began sending prophets to warn them of impending exile. This is the context in which the book of Jeremiah unfolds.

The Assyrians had already taken a large number of Israelites into exile, but not all of them. Jeremiah finds himself between the end of the Assyrian reign and the beginning of the exile to Babylon led by King Nebuchadnezzar. Jeremiah spends the majority of his writings pleading with the Israelites to repent and reconcile their relationship with God by turning from their ways and warning them of the seventy-year exile that would occur if they didn't. As Jeremiah predicted, they disregard the warnings and face exile. But God's many messages to the Israelites reveal His character, values, and the way He wants His people to live.

Thematically, the book of Jeremiah explores a multitude of topics, all of which are repeated and emphatically conveyed. We are encouraged that God knows us and wants to be in relationship with us, warning against polluting our minds by following false prophecies and worshiping false idols. There is a strict call to live our lives with justice, especially for the most vulnerable around us. He demonstrates how our pull to live self-sufficient lives is a form of disobedience and how we are called to live a life of radical repentance. He links intentional disobedience with the oppression of others and challenges all those who claim to follow Him to live true, godly lives with character and righteousness. Jeremiah can be a sobering book of the Bible to read, but by diving into it with an open heart to receive what He has for us, one can be encouraged and convicted to follow Him in more profound ways than ever experienced before.

Being Known

---✤---

What does it mean to "know" God? What does it mean to "know" each other? In our current vernacular, knowing someone typically means that you know of them. You know their name, and you might know details about their lives, like where they work, where they live, the names of their family members, etc. However, knowing someone as described in Scripture goes far beyond just intellectual knowledge. Truly knowing someone is relational. The Greek word for "knowing" is ginosko, which means "intimate, interactive, heart knowledge." Knowing each other is vital, but it must be based on a more secure premise than what we gain from one another. The Creator of the universe knows you.

He knows everything there is to learn about you. God is aware of every thought you've ever had, the motivations behind your actions, what you do, and why you do it. And He loves you anyway. Jeremiah 16:17 says, "My eyes are on all their ways; they are not hidden from me, nor is their sin concealed from my eyes." Every person alive is fully known by God, and yet that doesn't deter Him from unending compassion for them. There is often fear and trepidation that if someone truly knew you, they wouldn't love you. But that is exactly who Christ is. He knows you completely, and He loves you immeasurably more than you could ever fathom. And all He asks in return is that you would seek to know Him the same way that He knows you.

If we are all being honest, we really care about how much we are known, both positively and negatively. We love to be known for the good things we do, whether it is how we feel when someone unexpectedly remembers us or when we discover that others recognize something positive we've done in the past. On the other hand, it can be strange and frustrating when we feel like we should be known somewhere and we aren't, or when people know too much about us from social media without genuinely knowing us. Even worse is when people pretend to know you in order to gain something from you, but they actually do not know you at all. When we don't feel known or it is

18

cheap, it bothers us. As humans, at our core, we desire to be known by others and ultimately by our God.

David, who wrote Psalm 139, describes to what depth God knows us by saying, "O Lord, you have searched me, and you know me. You know when I sit and when I rise; you perceive my thoughts from afar. You discern my going out and my lying down; you are familiar with all my ways. Before a word is on my tongue, you know it completely, O Lord." We must embrace that we are fully known by the Father. When we accept the fact that God knows us, we have to ask the question, "What does it mean for us to know Him?"

In Jeremiah 22:15-17, he says, "Does it make you a king to have more and more cedar? Did not your father have food and drink? He did what was right and just, so all went well with him. He defended the cause of the poor and needy, and so all went well. Is that not what it means to know me?" declares the Lord. "But your eyes and your heart are set only on dishonest gain, on shedding innocent blood, and on oppression and extortion." God clearly links our depth of knowledge about Him to the practical application of how we live our lives. If we truly know Him, then our actions will demonstrate that knowledge. Jeremiah 17:10 says, "I, the Lord, search the heart and examine the mind to reward each person according to their conduct, according to what their deeds deserve."

Jeremiah builds on this thought in 9:23-24 by saying, "This is what the Lord says: 'Let not the wise boast of their wisdom or the strong boast of their strength or the rich boast of their riches, but let the one who boasts boast about this: that they have the understanding to know me, that I am the Lord, who exercises kindness, justice, and righteousness on earth, for in these I delight.'" Truly knowing God will impact how you live. You can't cognitively disassociate your knowledge of Him and your actions. And He says that when you know Him, you will live a life marked by kindness, justice, and righteousness. Many people claim to believe in God, but their actions don't reflect their profession.

James explains why it isn't good enough to just acknowledge that God is real when he says in James 2:19, "You believe that there is one God. Good! Even the demons believe that—and shudder." Even demons know that there is only one God. It isn't good enough to only know that God exists; you have to know him in the context of a relationship. It isn't just a one-time prayer. In Matthew 7:15-20, Jesus exclaims that his followers will be known by their fruit. A good tree cannot bear bad fruit, and a bad tree cannot bear good fruit. If we truly know Him, we will bear the fruit He describes, and that fruit comes from knowing Him.

We must engage in an active relationship, where we are seeking to know him more daily. Just like any other relationship, the more you pay attention to it, the more it will grow. And the more you ignore it, the more it will dissipate. God will never force Himself upon you, so when we seek Him, it creates real intimacy. True intimacy comes by choice. This is why God did not create us all to be mere instruments of worship. He could have easily created us in such a way that we didn't have a choice but to worship Him. When we choose to follow Him and get to know Him, the free will He gave us creates an intimacy that can't be formed in any other way.

Jeremiah reiterates multiple times throughout his writings that to be in a close relationship with us is his greatest desire. In 24:4-7 he says, "Then the Word of the Lord came to me: 'This is what the Lord, the God of Israel, says: "Like these good figs, I regard as good the exiles from Judah, whom I sent away from this place to the land of the Babylonians. My eyes will watch over them for their good, and I will bring them back to this land. I will build them up and not tear them down; I will plant them and not uproot them. I will give them a heart to know me, that I am the Lord. They will be my people, and I will be their God, for they will return to me with all their heart." and again in 30:22 when he says, "So you will be my people, and I will be your God." God's desire is for us to realize and accept that God fully knows us and loves us anyways. That love would then create a desire for us to get to know Him deeper. And through the outflow of that relationship, we would know others and allow others to know us.

Colossians 2:2 says, "... my purpose is that they may be encouraged in heart and united in love, so that they may have the full riches of complete understanding so that they may know the mystery of God." Knowing others and allowing yourself to be known is a core tenet of being in community. We intentionally seek to get to know those we are in close relationships with. This type of relationship is not a given; its existence is a choice. But being known and allowing yourself to be known come from a place of deep trust and intimacy.

The biggest benefit of allowing ourselves to be known in the context of community is that it gives us a true life of freedom. When you witness people find freedom from a life of secret sin, they all say the same thing. Once their sin was out in the open and they no longer had to hide, they found a freedom they didn't know existed. Scripture illustrates this event through one of the earliest accounts of human history: the time when Adam and Eve sinned and sought refuge in the garden. Even though God knew exactly where they were, He still asked where they were. That simple interaction shows the compassion and desire of God. By posing this question, He was extending an invitation to them to maintain their relationship with Him and reveal themselves once more. Knowing every aspect of yourself and having no secrets allows you to fully embrace life and follow God's path without any limitations.

We don't have to guess what it looks like for us to truly know Him, because His ways, desires, and law are given to us by Him. Reading His Word consistently is how we get to know Him better. However, He also forged it within us. Jeremiah 31:33 says, "This is the covenant I will make with the people of Israel after that time," declares the Lord. "I will put my law in their minds and write it on their hearts. I will be their God, and they will be my people." He created us with minds and hearts that can determine right from wrong. What is the fruit that should be coming from our lives if we truly know Him?

In Jeremiah, the prophet writes in many places throughout the book that dictate what a life should be marked by if someone knows God and follows Him. The prophet teaches us that pursuing His ways leads to a love for righteousness and justice. We stand up for those who are unable to defend themselves and show love to those who are unlovable. We live and work an honest life. We liberate the oppressed and safeguard life. An important aspect of life that Jeremiah mentions numerous times is that we are to treat people with fairness and compassion. If we don't have these traits, we aren't living as true followers of the Lord.

In the effort of being known and knowing others, we must start by embracing the fact that God knows us completely and loves us anyway. We are to build on that by getting to know Him as He knows us. This approach enables us to fully understand those close to us, develop a profound understanding of them, and maintain our identity in every situation we encounter. When we live our lives this way, we can answer the difficult question from Jeremiah 22:16 honestly: "Is that not what it means to know me?"

Questions to Ponder:

How does it feel knowing God knows everything there is to know about you? Why do you think you feel that way?

_____

_____

_____

_____

_____

_____

_____

_____

_____

Describe a situation where someone recognized you for a positive action you took, but you were unaware of their recognition.

_____

_____

_____

_____

_____

_____

_____

_____

_____

Describe a situation where someone knew you, and it made you uncomfortable because you felt they shouldn't have? How did that make you feel?

_____

_____

_____

_____

_____

_____

_____

_____

Why do you think "being known" is important to us as humans?

_____

_____

_____

_____

_____

_____

_____

_____

Why is knowing one another a core tenet of being in a community?

_____

_____

_____

_____

_____

_____

_____

_____

In the context of this chapter, how would you answer, "What does it mean to 'know' God?"

_____

_____

_____

_____

_____

_____

_____

_____

Idolatry and False Prophecies

When reading the entirety of Scripture, we see idolatry and false prophecy discussed in many passages. In our modern context, it is easy to believe that these are ancient struggles that we don't struggle with today. Long past are the days where people would worship wooden idols or stand in the streets and profess a glimpse into the future. Some might think that those issues are resolved. Or have they evolved into something new entirely?

Upon examining the foundations of idolatry and false prophecy, it becomes evident that neither has disappeared. They have just taken on a new form. Idolatry, simply put, is giving things/people the honor, prestige, and faith only reserved for God. Prophecy is simply speaking on behalf of God, and it becomes false when done for personal gain or human motives. Both missteps are not only present in our current society, but one could also argue that they are more prevalent now than any other time in history.

If idolatry is defined as something or someone that replaces God Himself, the screens in our lives provide the clearest representation of modern-day idolatry. The allure of what we watch, be it social media, YouTube, our favorite sports team, or a television show, consumes our lives. They consume our time and our thoughts and give us a place to escape rather than deal with the issues of the present age. We depend on distraction to alleviate our anxiety, worry, and stress instead of finding deliverance from the One who created us.

Just as those in Scripture would seek idols to help control aspects of their lives, the Western Church seeks deities to numb and comfort itself because of the lack of control they have over their lives. The heart of this age's idolatry is the same as always, though it looks different. The worst part of this paradigm is that we trade something holy and dynamic for something dead and worthless when we pursue idols instead of the Lord. Jeremiah 2:5 and 11 say, "This is what the Lord says: 'What fault did your ancestors find in me, that they strayed so far from me?' They followed worthless idols and became worthless themselves." "Has a nation ever changed its gods?" (Yet they are not gods at all.) But my people have exchanged their glorious God for worthless idols."

The Israelites that Jeremiah is speaking to are very familiar with physical idols. In this time, they lived in a polytheistic society, where people worshiped many false gods or idols. They would worship the "god" of the sea if they were fishing or the "god" of the moon, sun, or stars when they needed ideal weather, or even idols that were fashioned in the shape of animals to represent other false gods like Baal. All of this worship of false idols was a desperate attempt by man to help shape the future and prosperity of their lives here on earth. Sound familiar? The desire to bend the will of the cosmos to make life more comfortable or prosperous is an issue that has plagued mankind since sin entered the world. The issue was that, due to the idols' worthlessness and lack of the power mankind so desperately sought, their prayers and idolatrous worship would be met with deafening silence.

Jeremiah 2:27-28 demonstrates this conundrum when God says, "They say to wood, 'You are my father,' and to stone, 'You gave me birth.' They have turned their backs on me and not their faces; yet when they are in trouble, they say, 'Come and save us!' Where then are the gods you made for yourselves? Let them come if they can save you when you are in trouble! For you, Judah, have as many gods as you have towns." There is only one God who hears, sees, and delivers. And it was never something fashioned by man. Only those who acknowledge God's power and reject the enticing temptation of false idols are truly delivered. Since the beginning of time, people have observed that seeking deliverance from anything or anyone apart from God consistently fails, yet we persistently believe that if we "achieve that one more thing," things will turn out differently this time. However, not getting our way is not the only consequence of pursuing false idols instead of God Himself.

"When you tell these people all this and they ask you, 'Why has the Lord decreed such a great disaster against us? What wrong have we done? What sin have we committed against the Lord our God?' Then say to them, 'It is because your ancestors forsook me,' declares the Lord, 'and followed other gods and served and worshiped them. They forsook me and did not keep my law. But you have behaved more wickedly than your ancestors. See how all of you are following the stubbornness of your evil hearts instead of obeying me. So, I will throw you out of this land into a land neither you nor your ancestors have known, and there you will serve other gods day and night, for I will show you no favor.'" What Jeremiah 16:10-13 shows us is how personally God takes it when we seek anything that is supposed to come from Him. Whether that is deliverance, joy, comfort, or wisdom, whenever we place something or someone above Him, that is idolatry.

And as we see from the example of the Israelites, sometimes in our broken human state, we don't even see it in our own lives.

They ask the question, "Why are all these things happening to us?" and "What have we done wrong, or how have we sinned?" Yet, their sin is blatantly obvious. Is it not also evident in our lives? They fell out of God's favor because they forsook Him. To forsake is to abandon, renounce, or give up something or someone valuable. They did this by following other gods, serving and worshiping them instead of God Himself. They behaved wickedly and followed their own stubborn, evil hearts instead of depending on Him for direction. They couldn't see it in themselves due to the blindness that accompanies sin, but it was clear why they were experiencing what they were.

The thing about following false idols or the direction of our heart and will is that it is deceiving. In Jeremiah 17:9, it says, "The heart is deceitful above all things, and desperately sick; who can understand it?" Doing what you want, as the world says, will lead to evil. The extent of this evil is illustrated in Jeremiah 7:31, which states, "They have built the high places of Topheth in the Valley of Ben Hinnom to burn their sons and daughters in the fire—something I did not command, nor did it enter my mind." These people were literally sacrificing and burning their

31

children alive because it is what false idols or their flesh told them to do.

The Israelites show us an obvious example of what happens when we rely on false idols to deliver us instead of depending on the Creator of the Universe. But their tragedy doesn't stop them from wallowing in self-pity and wondering what they could have done to avoid it. In chapter 22:8-9 of Jeremiah, the Lord responds, stating, "People from many nations will pass by this city and will ask one another, 'Why has the Lord done such a thing to this great city?'" The answer is, "Because they have forsaken the covenant of the Lord, their God, and have worshiped and served other gods." Who you follow and listen to for guidance is incredibly important. And whether that is from our flesh, some idol in our lives, or from other people, it is clear that God is a jealous god. Some try to speak on behalf of God and guide His people, but as we see in Scripture, their efforts can go awry, too.

Worshipping and depending on a false idol, especially in biblical times, was an obvious violation of God's commandments. But one area that was much more convoluted and gray was his use of prophets. When one hears the word "prophet," they almost always immediately conjure thoughts of someone prophetically telling the future of what is to come. That can be a component of someone who is a prophet; however, a prophet is simply defined as someone who speaks on behalf of God. The most common use of prophecy in Scripture is when a prophet pleads with Israel to repent from their sin. And when God uses a prophet in this manner, one must obey. However, there are many instances throughout the Bible where individuals, both intentionally and unintentionally in their strength, with their motives and direction, mislead the Israelites by claiming their words are coming from the One true God, but instead they were coming from themselves.

Much like idolatry, people have become convinced over time that the issue of false prophecy is reserved for Bible times and doesn't appear in today's modern era. This belief is utterly false. The issue of false prophecy has rapidly expanded, especially in the era of social media and the ability to instantly share ideas with millions without considering the potential repercussions. The main issue with false prophecy, is when you claim to speak on behalf of God, but you aren't, that is blasphemy which has dire consequences. There is credence to the thought that when you "say the Lord's name in vain," it occurs when you exclaim Jesus' name as a curse word. But the much deeper version of saying the Lord's name in vain is when you attribute something to Him without it being so.

We see in the Old Testament that the penalty for being a false prophet is literally death. No one is advocating for that consequence to be applied today for falsely speaking on behalf of God, but it does illustrate the seriousness with which God regards this issue. In Jeremiah 28:15-17, there is an account of Hananiah, who was guilty of this. "Then the prophet Jeremiah said to Hananiah the prophet, "Listen, Hananiah! The Lord has not sent you, yet you have persuaded this nation to trust in lies. Therefore, this is what the Lord says: 'I am about to remove you from the face of the earth. This very year you are going to die, because you have preached rebellion against the Lord.'" In the seventh month of that same year, Hananiah the prophet died." Jeremiah rebukes the false prophet Hananiah because he persuaded the nation to trust in lies, and his consequence was quite literally death.

It is easy to see accounts like this and shrug them off as someone who wasn't a follower of God and was attempting to mislead His people intentionally. But Jeremiah makes it obvious throughout the book that the most dangerous false prophets of his era and ours are people who claim to be people of God, even those deemed "shepherds" of His people. Jeremiah 50:6-7 clearly says, "My people have been lost sheep; their shepherds have led them astray and caused them to roam on the mountains. They wandered over mountain and hill and forgot their resting place. Whoever found them devoured them; their enemies said, "We are not guilty, for they sinned against the Lord, their true pasture, the Lord, the hope of their ancestors."

25:34-35 says, "Weep and wail, you shepherds; roll in the dust, you leaders of the flock. The moment for your slaughter has arrived; you will plummet like the finest rams. The shepherds will have nowhere to flee, the leaders of the flock no place to escape." And the Lord declares, "Woe to the shepherds who are destroying and scattering the sheep of my pasture!" in 23:1. It is people claiming to be of God who were and are leading the sheep to slaughter. Other places in Scripture say that there will be "wolves, dressed in sheep's clothing," but what Jeremiah is describing is an environment where it isn't even sheep that are being misled; it will be shepherds who were tasked with taking care of the sheep!

In a time where conspiracy theories, half-truths, and fearmongering run rampant, it has never been easier for false prophets to run rampant. Where people are convinced by scriptures being used out of context, "signs" from half-baked interpretations of the end times, and "dreams and visions" being communicated as direct words from the Lord, it is no surprise that the sheep have been led astray. Here's the hard truth that most people don't want to hear: Yes, prophecy is real, and God will speak to people directly through a myriad of methods. However, if one of their words is ever wrong, even once, that means that they are listening to false spirits or their flesh. Period. We cannot undervalue this. An individual must always remain correct to be a genuine prophet from

God and avoid being labeled a "false prophet." Some people confuse the gift of prophecy and the gift of knowledge given to believers by the Holy Spirit. But they could not be more different.

The gift of knowledge is where the Holy Spirit gives us divine insight or knowledge about someone that will help us love them, lead them, or call them to repentance. But sometimes those words are partial, don't provide a full context, or are only meant for certain circumstances. So, when someone has the gift of knowledge, sometimes they can be wrong or maybe not have the full picture and still be operating from a place of divine insight. But when someone claims that a "word is from the Lord" and is utilizing the gift of prophecy, that means that word is directly from Him and therefore would never be wrong. This distinction is important because one gives room for misinterpretation or misapplication, and the other has very severe consequences if proven incorrect. You generally (not always) can tell right away if a word is from the Lord or if it is from man by figuring out whom the word serves.

Jeremiah 28:9 plainly backs this thought up by stating, "But the prophet who prophesies peace will be recognized as one truly sent by the Lord only if his prediction comes true." When a word is given and it leads to repentance, reconciliation, and peace, when looking at the entirety of the words given in Scripture, that generally means it is in the right direction. However, there are times that we also see in the Bible where words from the Lord are about the destruction of people, cities, or towns, and He is communicating that through a prophet. Chapter 38, verses 1-4 of Jeremiah, shows us an example of this when it says, "Shephatiah son of Mattan, Gedaliah son of Pashhur, Jehukal son of Shelemiah, and Pashhur son of Malkijah heard what Jeremiah was telling all the people when he said, 'This is what the Lord says: Whoever stays in this city will die by the sword, famine, or plague, but whoever goes over to the Babylonians will live. They will escape with their lives; they will live. And this is what the Lord says: 'This city will certainly be given into the hands of the army of the king of Babylon, who will capture it.'" Then the officials said to the king, "This man should be put to death. He is discouraging the soldiers who are left in this city, as well as all the people, with the things he is saying to them. This man is not seeking the good of these people but their ruin." Even though it wasn't a positive word, Jeremiah still boldly spoke it, and the people rejected it because it didn't lead to favorable results for them. However, we take solace in the fact that when God gives us words of prophecy, it is to reconcile our relationship with Him and lead us where He wants us to go.

Jeremiah points out that false prophets will often use fear to manipulate people to gain a following. This can be seen in chapter 23:3-4 which says, "Therefore this is what the Lord, the God of Israel, says to the shepherds who tend my people, "Because you have scattered my flock and driven them away and have not bestowed care on them, I will bestow punishment on you for the evil you have done," declares the Lord. "I will gather the remnant of my flock out of all the countries where I have driven them and will bring them back to their pasture, where they will be fruitful and increase in number. The Lord says, "I will appoint shepherds to care for them, and they will no longer be afraid or lost." We can trust that God's words are true and will come to pass. Solomon in Proverbs 30:5-6 points to the truth when he writes, "Every word of God is flawless; He is a shield to those who take refuge in him. Do not add to his words, or he will rebuke you and prove you a liar." We should not take lightly those who lie and claim to represent God, as they face severe consequences.

God's own words to Jeremiah in 27:9-10 & 15 outline the severity with which God treats those who take His name in vain and speak false words on His behalf when He says, "So do not listen to your prophets, your diviners, your interpreters of dreams, your mediums, or your sorcerers who tell you, 'You will not serve the king of Babylon.' They deceive you, promising exile, banishment, and death. – 'I have not sent them,' declares the Lord. They are prophesying lies in my name. Therefore, I will banish you, and you will perish, both you and the prophets who prophesy to you." The passage continues in 14:14-16, stating, "Then the Lord said to me, The prophets are prophesying lies in my name. I have not sent them, appointed them, or spoken to them. They are prophesying to you false visions, divinations, idolatries, and the delusions of their minds. Therefore, this is what the Lord says about the prophets who are prophesying in my name: I did not send them, yet they are saying, 'No sword or famine will touch this land.' Those same prophets will perish by sword and famine. The famine and sword will drive the people they prophesy for into the streets of Jerusalem. There will be no one to bury them or their families. I will pour out on them the calamity they deserve." If you didn't know the extent of evil, a false word from a prophet, you do now.

We live in an age where people can create a YouTube channel, garner thousands, if not millions, of followers and views, and say whatever they want to. And especially in 2020, we saw the rise of many false prophets who spoke to "what would happen" following the election in the United States, and so many were proven incorrect. And yet, were these people rebuked and chastised for being wrong? No, they weren't. People continued listening to them and hanging on every word of what the future could hold, and they remain influential today. These aren't just people on the outskirts of Evangelicalism; these are influential pastors, deacons, and content creators who thrive off of fearmongering and "words from the Lord" that fall flat each time the day or hour their word is meant to pass. This kind of behavior isn't a new phenomenon; in Jeremiah 23:10-11, he says, "The land is full of adulterers; because of the curse, the land lies parched and the pastures in the wilderness are withered." The prophets follow an evil course and use their power unjustly. "Both the prophet and priest are godless; even in my temple, I find their wickedness, declares the Lord." But we see a continual refusal in the body of Christ to rebuke these people/channels as false prophets. We lack the conviction to hold these people to account and stop consuming their content. Whether it is for entertainment or spiritual guidance, what these people are doing is wicked and blasphemous. If you don't believe the seriousness with which God takes it, take His own word for it:

"Do not heed the prophets; they give you false hope," says the Lord. They speak visions from their minds, not from the mouth of the Lord. They keep saying to those who despise me, 'The Lord says you will have peace.' And to all who follow the stubbornness of their hearts, they say, 'No harm will come to you.' But which of them has stood at the council of the Lord to see or hear his word? Who has listened and heard his word? See, the storm of the Lord will burst out in wrath, a whirlwind swirling down on the heads of the wicked. The anger of the Lord will not turn back until he fully accomplishes the purposes of his heart. In days to come, you will understand it clearly. I did not send these prophets, yet they have run with their message; I did not speak to them, yet they have prophesied. If they were on my council, they would have preached my words to my people and turned them from sin. "Am I only a God nearby," declares the Lord, "and not a God far away? Who can hide in secret places so that I cannot see them?" declares the Lord. "Do not I fill heaven and earth?" declares the Lord. "I have heard the words of the prophets who prophesy lies in my name. They say, 'I had a dream! I had a dream!' How long will such deception continue in the hearts of these lying prophets, who prophesy the delusions of their minds? They think the dreams they tell one another will make my people forget my name, just as their ancestors forgot my name through Baal worship. Let the prophet tell his dream, but let the one who has my word speak it. What does straw have to do with grain?" declares the Lord. "My word is like fire," declares the Lord, "and like a hammer that breaks a rock into pieces. Therefore, I am against the prophets who steal words from one another, claiming they are from me." Yes," declares the Lord, "I am against the prophets who wag their tongues and yet declare, 'The Lord declares.' Indeed, I am against those who prophesy false dreams," declares the Lord. "They tell false dreams and lead my people astray with their reckless lies, yet I did not send or appoint them. They do not benefit these people in the least," declares the Lord."

When people speak false words, it is always self-serving. Whether it is building their influence or trying to advance in a worldly sense, it becomes obvious that they were never speaking on behalf of God, just using His name to achieve their own will. This form of spiritual abuse affects not only those with large audiences but also individuals in smaller contexts. When someone uses God's name casually to persuade another person to take action, it is considered evil and blasphemous. The exploitation of individuals by using God's name has been occurring since the beginning of time. In Jeremiah 23:36, it says, "But you must not mention a message from the Lord again, because each one's word becomes their message." So you distort the words of the living God, the Lord Almighty, our God." There have been and continue to be people who will use the Lord's name to achieve personal accomplishments built on falsehood. Flee from these people, renounce them, and do not give them a platform. That said, some people are true prophets who hear from the Lord, and we must heed their words.

Examples of people who heard from prophets sent by the Lord and chose to disobey are abundant in the Bible. They often killed prophets for what they said, which they considered blasphemous. Jeremiah 44:4-6 dictates God's response to those people when it says, "Again and again I sent my servants the prophets, who said, 'Do not do this detestable thing that I hate!' But they did not listen or pay attention; they did not turn from their wickedness or stop burning incense to other gods. So my wrath was unleashed on the towns of Judah and the streets of Jerusalem, leaving them in ruins." It is virtuous to hear words that are from God and obey them. But how do you tell the difference?

There is no simple way to determine whether something comes from God or not when it comes to a prophet speaking. But first, you compare it to what God says in the Bible and who you know Him to be. A clear word that contradicts God's character immediately raises a red flag. Or if there are passages in the Bible that contradict what is being spoken, we know that God doesn't contradict Himself and that He is unchanging. And lastly, we can ask the Holy Spirit to give us wisdom and discernment while testing the word given against all of these things. After reading Jeremiah, we see that we must take the Lord's prophetic words seriously. But what if you have fallen prey to ill-spoken words? What if you experienced conviction regarding idols in your life that have replaced God?

God's mercy is available; all He asks of us is to repent. If we are caught worshiping false idols, all we have to do is remind ourselves where our hope lies. Jeremiah encourages us to do this in 14:22 when he says, "Do any of the worthless idols of the nations bring rain? Do the skies themselves send down showers? No, it is you, Lord our God. Therefore, our hope is in you, for you are the one who does all this." There is a path for us to follow that requires humility, honesty, and a commitment to follow truth. "If you, Israel, will return, then return to me," declares the Lord. "If you put your detestable idols out of my sight and no longer go astray, and if, in a truthful, just, and righteous way, you swear, 'As surely as the Lord lives,' then the nations will invoke blessings from him, and in him they will boast." Jeremiah 4:1-2

Return to the Lord by denouncing idols, staying faithful, and acknowledging God's existence in a truthful, just, and righteous way. Check all words given to believers through the wisdom and discernment of the Holy Spirit and the truth of His word. And lean on Him as the ultimate source of truth, comfort, and guidance for our lives.

Questions to Ponder:

What does idolatry look like in our modern era?

_____

_____

_____

_____

_____

_____

_____
_____

When we follow false idols instead of God, how do you think that makes Him feel?

_____
_____
_____
_____
_____
_____
_____
_____

Explain how saying you are speaking on behalf of God when you aren't is taking the Lord's name in vain.

_____
_____
_____
_____
_____
_____
_____
_____

Why is false prophecy dangerous?

_____
_____

_____

_____

_____

_____

_____

_____

Why do you think God takes people blaspheming His name in this way so seriously?

_____

_____

_____

_____

_____

_____

_____

_____

What are the characteristics of false words, and how can you identify them?

_____

_____

_____

_____

_____

_____

_____

_____

Why is it important for us to be mindful, prayerful, and wise when we "speak on behalf of God"?

_____

_____

_____

_____

_____

_____

_____

_____

_____

Why is it crucial that we speak on God's behalf when He asks us to?

_____

_____

_____

_____

_____

_____

_____

_____

Justice

———— ❧ ————

Spending any length of time with children reveals an innate sense of justice in humanity. They desire to see immediate consequences for those who have done wrong and may even seek revenge as a way to enforce their sense of justice. This phenomenon explains why countless individuals have grappled with a world that appears to lack justice throughout history. They'll ask themselves questions like, "Why is it that the most corrupt among us tend to be more successful than the righteous?" Or, "If God is just, why does He allow wickedness to transpire?" One might contemplate, "Are the negative outcomes in my life happening because God is carrying out justice?" These questions are nothing new. Many will ask these questions after us, as those before us did. But rest assured,

God has plenty to say about justice and what it looks like in this broken world.

In the book of Jeremiah, as a whole, God is telling the Israelites that how they are living is wicked, which bears consequences. He is exhorting them to repent, return to Him, and live with justice and righteousness among His people. Of course, they don't obey, but this prophetic message has all the markings of His justice. It is wrapped up in truth, consequence, and compassion.

In reality, God consistently upholds righteousness. Always. Jeremiah echoes a common frustration that many humans have experienced in chapter 12:1: "You are always righteous, Lord, when I bring a case before you." Yet I would speak with you about your justice: Why does the way of the wicked prosper? Why do all the faithless live at ease?" And the answer that He gives us doesn't fully address our concerns. The answer is that we must have faith in His sovereignty, understanding that God does not guarantee His faithful followers prosperity in the world's definition. In fact, in most places, especially in the life and teachings of Jesus, we see the opposite. We expect to face adversity, persecution, and hardship in our earthly lives as Christians. Despite that truth, He is still who He says He is.

David accurately describes God in Psalm 11:7 when he says, "For the Lord is righteous, He loves justice; the upright will see his face." Whether it is within our physical lifetimes on earth or before the judgment seat at the end of days, God's justice is present and eternal. We cannot confuse the lack of physical abundance on earth as a sign of God's apathy, in the same way that we shouldn't confuse earthly riches as confirmation of God's approval. Physical outcomes are not always a sign of God's justice or lack thereof, but occasionally they are.

We do see in many instances that God does exact his form of perfect justice in the moment for those who live unrighteously. But not always. In Jeremiah 21:10, it says, "I have determined to do this city harm and not good, declares the Lord. It will be given into the hands of the king of Babylon, and he will destroy it with fire." And later in chapter 21, verse 14 says, "I will punish you as your deeds deserve, declares the Lord. I will ignite a fire in your forests, consuming everything in its path." God sees the injustice and the unrighteousness. And when we see Him choose to take action against it, there are severe consequences to those who find themselves in the ire of His gaze. There are many instances in both the Old and the New Testament where God carries out His form of justice because of grotesque disobedience or abundant wickedness. In the days of Noah, the wickedness was so perverse and widespread that the Lord decided to essentially start over with humanity. Granted, He promised He would never flood the earth again in the form of a rainbow, but that is still an example of God carrying out physical justice as a consequence for wickedness. Physical harm or hardship can be a form of God's justice in your life, but it also could just be a product of living in a broken and sinful world. The times that it is God's direct hand at work seem few and far between in Scripture.

The key to understanding God's justice in its many forms is trusting that if it is God's justice being poured out on your life, it is with a desire to bring you back to Him. In Jeremiah 46:28, it says, "Do not be afraid, Jacob my servant, for I am with you," declares the Lord. "Though I completely destroy all the nations among which I scatter you, I will not completely destroy you. I will discipline you, but only with justice; I will not let you go entirely unpunished." But what type of wickedness does God take immediate action against?

In the book of Jeremiah, God declares through the prophet that there are specific reasons why He would carry out justice among His people. The first reason is His distaste for individuals who amass wealth at the expense of those unable to defend themselves and who acquire wealth through unfair methods. Chapter 22:13 of Jeremiah says, "Woe to him who builds his palace by unrighteousness, his upper rooms by injustice, making his own people work for nothing, not paying them for their labor," and it is emphasized in 17:11 when he says, "Like a partridge that hatches eggs it did not lay are those who gain riches by unjust means. When their lives are half gone, their riches will desert them, and in the end they will prove to be fools."

Jeremiah also gives a tangible example of this unrighteousness in Chapter 34:12-16, "Then the word of the Lord came to Jeremiah: "This is what the Lord, the God of Israel, says: I made a covenant with your ancestors when I brought them out of Egypt, out of the land of slavery. I said, 'Every seventh year, each of you must free any fellow Hebrews who have sold themselves to you.' After they have served you six years, you must let them go free.' Your ancestors, however, did not listen to me or pay attention to me. Recently, you repented and did what is right in my sight: each of you proclaimed freedom to your people. You even made a covenant before me in the house that bears my name. But now you've turned around and profaned my name; you've taken back the male and female slaves you had freed. You have forced them to become your slaves again."

God specifically cares about how we treat those whom we are responsible for. In this case, he is referring to slaves, who, at that time, were only held to six years of service if they had sold themselves into servitude. He told them to let them go in year seven, but they didn't listen. The Lord cares about how we treat, talk to, pay, and release people. This is just one way that the Lord holds us accountable for our interactions with others.

He calls us to protect those who cannot protect themselves. Demonstrating this stance, Jeremiah 22:3 says, "This is what the Lord says: Do what is just and right. Rescue from the hands of the oppressor— the one who has been robbed. Do no wrong or violence to the foreigner, the fatherless, or the widow, and do not shed innocent blood in this place." That list of people is wrapped up in decades worth of political tangles in the West. It is not politically advantageous to tell Christians they need to rescue people from oppression. Or to treat foreigners with dignity and respect. Caring for widows and orphans who are easily cast aside. Protecting all life that is innocent. Even as these items are listed, as one reads it, they feel a ping inside their spirit because of the political dissension that accompanies them.

Regardless of what has been debated or said, God is clear throughout Scripture that followers of "The Way" are called to those mandates. It does not matter which political party decides to carry the cause of any of the classes listed that day; Christians are charged with the task of doing what is just and right. You can choose to join God, but that won't stop Him from doing so. "Sing to the Lord! Praise the Lord! He rescues the lives of the needy from the hands of the wicked." Jeremiah 20:13

The Lord is just in all of His ways. Going back to David, he writes in Psalm 89:14, "Righteousness and justice are the foundation of your throne; love and faithfulness go before you." Righteousness and justice are the foundation of His throne. We must trust that He is in control. He is sovereign and all knowing. Leaning into the knowledge that He is faithful and worthy to be praised. In Jeremiah 31:27-28, He outlines it perfectly by saying, "The days are coming, declares the Lord," "when I will plant the kingdoms of Israel and Judah with the offspring of people and animals. Just as I watched over them to uproot and tear down and to overthrow, destroy, and bring disaster, so I will watch over them to build and to plant, declares the Lord."

There is a time to be uprooted, torn down, and overthrown. But there is also a time to build and to plant. And whether we find ourselves in situations of hardship or plentiful abundance, neither is a clear sign of God's justice or lack thereof. When God carries out justice, it is always with the thought in mind that the consequences would draw people closer to Himself. The Lord's justice is directly linked with His compassion. In Jeremiah 33:26b it says, "For I will restore their fortunes and have compassion on them." And that compassion leads to Him carrying out justice on our behalf. It is never our role to be the arbiter of justice, unless he commands it. In 2 Thessalonians 1:6 it says, "God is just: He will pay back trouble to those who trouble you." It may not happen on our timeline or how we would like to see it done. It may be in this life or at the judgment seat, but either way, we must trust that God's version of justice is righteous and pure, whereas ours can be marred by hurt, selfishness, greed, or any number of things.

The question of why God allows "bad" things to happen to "good" people is lacking a true premise to begin with. Living in a broken and sinful world means that hardship and trials will inevitably come to all people. Matthew 5:44-46 says, "But I tell you, love your enemies and pray for those who persecute you, that you may be children of your Father in heaven. He causes His sun to rise on the evil and the good and sends rain on the righteous and the unrighteous. If you love those who love you, what reward will you get? Aren't tax collectors also doing that?" No matter how well we live, we will all lose loved ones and face trials. On the opposite side of that question is the belief that somehow there are people who are inherently "good." Romans 3 counters that thought in verses 21-24 when it says, "But now, apart from the law, the righteousness of God has been made known, to which the law and the prophets testify. This righteousness is given through faith in Jesus Christ to all who believe. There is no difference between Jew and Gentile, for all have sinned and fallen short of the glory of God, and all are justified freely by His grace through the redemption that came by Christ Jesus." There is not one of us who could achieve eternity with Him on our own merits. This belief implies that there are no "good" or "bad" individuals, only sinners in need of grace and forgiveness. It's normal to question the reasons for our struggles, but it doesn't mean you're not "good" in God's eyes.

The abundance of the wicked is not a commentary on their righteousness, in the same way that someone's poverty is not an indication of their wickedness. God is just, and He is sovereign. All He asks of us is to trust that no matter what physical situation we find ourselves in, His justice is good.

Questions to Ponder:

How would you answer someone if they asked you, "Why does God allow "bad" things to happen to "good" people?"

_____
_____
_____
_____
_____
_____
_____
_____

Why is it wrong to take justice into our own hands outside of the leading of God?

_____
_____

_____
_____
_____
_____
_____
_____

How is the lack of physical abundance not a sign of God's apathy?

_____
_____
_____
_____
_____
_____
_____
_____

How are earthly riches not a confirmation of God's approval?

_____
_____
_____
_____
_____
_____

_____

_____

What type of sin does God seem to emphasize most when taking immediate action?

_____

_____

_____

_____

_____

_____

_____

_____

_____

_____

What classes of people does God specifically call those who claim to follow Him to care for and protect?

_____

_____

_____

_____

_____

_____

_____

Self-Sufficiency

Individualism is the inescapable default within Western society. The willingness to "pull yourself up by your bootstraps" and live the "American Dream" is drilled into our heads from a young age. Pride emanates from those who claim to "do it by themselves" despite others doubting them and the ability to "bet on yourself" in situations where everything works against you. These principles are widely shared and agreed upon in modern society as moral high ground and what most seek to achieve. When someone bucks against this ideology, it shakes the very bedrock of how our society operates. Which is why it should be problematic to read Scripture and find that none of those principles are anywhere to be found.

Oftentimes, people will confuse inspirational quotes with the teachings of Jesus. People frequently use a quote that Jesus never said: "God will help those who help themselves." In fact, not only did He never say that, but he taught the exact opposite. Saying things like, "Come to me, all you who are weary and burdened, and I will give you rest." Take my yoke upon you and learn from me, for I am gentle and humble in heart, and you will find rest for your souls. For my yoke is easy and my burden is light," in Matthew 11:28-30. And it wasn't just Jesus. In the Old Testament, Solomon says in Proverbs 3:5-6, "Trust in the Lord with all your heart and lean not on your own understanding; in all your ways submit to Him, and He will make your paths straight."

Jeremiah speaks at length in Chapter 17 when he draws the comparison between those dependent on men instead of trusting in Him. Verse 5 says, "This is what the Lord says: 'Cursed is the one who trusts in man, who draws strength from mere flesh, and whose heart turns away from the Lord." And in direct contrast, a couple of verses later, in verses 7 and 8 when he says, "But blessed is the one who trusts in the Lord, whose confidence is in him. They will be like a tree planted by the water that sends out its roots by the stream. It does not fear when heat comes; its leaves are always green. It has no worries in a year of drought and never fails to bear fruit."

Self-sufficiency is a sin. It is an attempt to construct an idol of self so large that God is no longer needed. This type of sin is characterized by a belief that one has more control over their own destiny than God does and a reluctance to adhere to His will for their life. Jeremiah outlines such an attitude clearly in 2:13 & 17 when he says, "My people have committed two sins: They have forsaken me, the spring of living water, and have dug their own cisterns, broken cisterns that cannot hold water." – "Have you not brought this tragedy on yourselves by forsaking the Lord your God when he led you in the way?" It is a sin to forsake God by doing things in our strength when He has given us a way. As he points out, it's one thing to act in your strength and a whole different issue when He does give guidance and you choose to do something of your volition.

In 1 Peter 2:21, Peter echoes these points by saying, "It would have been better for them not to have known the way of righteousness than to have known it and then to turn their backs on the sacred command that was passed on to them." The Lord, through Jeremiah, is even stronger in this sentiment when He says, "This is what the Lord Almighty, the God of Israel, says: 'Listen! I am going to bring on this city and all the villages around it every disaster I pronounced against them, because they were stiff-necked and would not listen to my words." Jeremiah 19:15. There are times that we say we want the Lord to lead us, but when He does, we still don't listen. In reality, we merely expect the Lord to validate our aspirations and goals, but He has His own unique vision and plan for our lives. And when we find out that it can be contrary to our own thoughts, we rely on our strength and trust ourselves more than Him.

The Lord's most frustrating part of this dynamic is that He freely provides guidance when asked, as He did for the Israelites. In Jeremiah 6:16, he exclaims his frustration when he says, "This is what the Lord says: 'Stand at the crossroads and look; ask for the ancient paths, ask where the right way is, and walk in it, and you will find rest for your souls. But you said, "We will not walk in it." As God's people, we have the freedom to seek the right path and follow it, with the assurance that we will find rest. Israel knew the right path but said, "We will not walk in it." Too often, especially in Western society, instead of leaning into God's leading, we trust in our abundance to take care of us. In Jeremiah 48:7, the Lord confronted Moab for his similar idolatry, warning him, "Because you trust in your deeds and riches, you too will be taken captive, and Chemosh will go into exile, along with his priests and officials." Moab learned that deeds and riches can only take you so far.

When our faith in our comprehension inevitably falters and life becomes challenging, the formula remains unchanged since the beginning of time. We cry out to the

Lord. Israel repeatedly cries out to the Lord throughout the Old Testament, a practice that even the disciples and the early church emulated. We'd rather trust in our wisdom, our riches, and our own selfish motives than rely on the authority of God until we are placed in a situation where we need deliverance from Him. Chapter 21 of Jeremiah is an entire section of Scripture dedicated to Zedekiah crying out to the one true God only when he needs something. Nebuchadnezzar was attacking them in this specific case, and only divine intervention from the Lord could save them. How often are we all guilty of this? We often assume control and tell the Lord, "We can handle this," rather than relying on Him, His presence, and His guidance. Eventually, we find ourselves in a difficult situation, and then we rely on Him to rescue us from our mess. Sound familiar?

In Jeremiah 22:21, God names this dynamic when He says, "I warned you when you felt secure, but you said, 'I will not listen!' This mindset has been your way from your youth; you have not obeyed me." Notice that He mentions a time when you felt secure. He observes and understands that our vulnerability is greatest when we place our trust in our own strength. Whether it is the size of our 401k, where we are at in our careers, relationships, or positions, whenever we stop depending on the Lord and begin trusting our strength instead, we disobey God. The sad part is that we all inherently know that we should trust in the Lord above ourselves, but whether it is pride, ego, disillusionment, or ignorance, all of us still struggle to some degree with doing things in our strength instead of His. Such trust is especially misguided when understanding our place in the cosmos.

God created the entire universe and even says bluntly, "I am the Lord, the God of all mankind. Is anything too difficult for me?" in Jeremiah 32:27. Despite acknowledging and praising Him for it, we continue to pursue self-sufficiency. Self-help books fly off the shelves, whole podcasts exist, and entire industries have been created in pursuit of self-sufficiency because it is praised so widely, making it difficult to escape in Western culture. This is a sin that most, if not all, people who live in the West struggle with and yet rarely talk about. So, how do we begin living our lives fully dependent on the Lord instead of our strength?

First, we need to be honest. In Jeremiah 14:7, the Israelites are forthright when they say, "Although our sins testify against us, do something, Lord, for the sake of your name. For our backsliding is great; we have sinned against you." Backsliding is an accurate word to describe this phenomenon. Whenever we witness the Lord delivering us in mighty ways and reflect on our past ineptitude, we exclaim, "Why didn't we just trust the Lord to begin with?" And with that epiphany, we become determined not to make that mistake again. But alas, time goes on, we begin to see success build in areas of our lives that we give ourselves more credit than we should, and the cycle continues. The heart of the Lord is always to draw us closer to Him. The second thing we do when we find ourselves caught up in our self-sufficiency is to live a life of radical repentance. Our honesty leads to true confession, which turns into repentance and a willingness to turn the other way. If we humbly accept this correction and repent whenever it arises, it will gradually diminish in our lives.

Lastly, we need to lean into the restoration that the Lord offers us. In Jeremiah 27:22, it says, "'They will be taken to Babylon, and there they will remain until the day I come for them,' declares the Lord. 'Then I will bring them back and restore them to this place.'" Restoration and reconciliation are the goal of any true repentance. To bring the relationship back to a repaired place that can be built upon. And that place is a constant state of dependence on the Lord. God desires to do life with you, providing vision, direction, wisdom, discernment, and calling, along with everything else in between. In our self-absorbed, self-sufficient mentality, we become convinced that we need to do this life for God. In actuality, God's primary aspiration is to share this life with us.

Questions to Ponder:

Why is 'self-sufficiency' a sin?

_____

_____

_____

_____

_____

_____

_____

Why is it worse to know the leading of God and then not follow it?

_____

_____

_____

_____

_____

_____

_____

_____

_____

Explain the cycle that we've seen since the beginning of time as it pertains to 'self-sufficiency.'

_____

_____

_____

_____

_____

_____

_____

_____

What promises does God give revolving around the leading of His people?

_____

_____

_____

_____

_____

_____

_____

_____

Why does God continue to rescue us, even when we follow our own hearts/desires?

_____

_____

_____

_____

_____

_____

_____

_____

When are believers most vulnerable? Why is that?

_____

_____

_____

_____

_____

_____

_____

_____

_____

_____

_____

_____

Unrepentance

───────── ❧ ─────────

Being called a "stiff-necked" person is not a common phrase heard today. But the people who are described that way in Scripture can be seen all over the place and in ourselves. It is used to describe the Israelites when they were unrepentant. One could say that Jeremiah was sent to the Israelites because they were obstinate.

The reason why unrepentance is so offensive to God is that it is a choice. When we make mistakes or sin, there are times we commit those offenses by accident or by happenstance. There is grace for that. However, within that grace, all the Lord asks for us to do in these moments is to confess, repent, reconcile, and obey. As we see with the Israelites as a prime example of what not to do, despite prophets and words being sent to them, they continue in their ways. There is a type of arrogant pride that rears its ugly head when someone's sin is exposed, and yet they refuse to acknowledge it. In Jeremiah 7:28, he describes not only their disobedience but also their actions after it was exposed when he says, "Therefore say to them, 'This is the nation that has not obeyed the Lord its God or responded to correction. Truth has perished; it has vanished from their lips."

Even when the Lord corrects them with physical consequences, they don't respond. In chapter 5, verse 3, it says, "Lord, do not your eyes look for truth? You struck them, but they felt no pain; you crushed them, but they refused correction. They made their faces harder than stone and refused to repent." They deliberately chose not to repent, "hardening" their faces and rejecting correction. Despite constant warnings, calls to return, and offerings of grace and mercy, they exasperate the Lord by their unwillingness to respond in kind.

The Old and New Testaments explicitly refer to this as "wickedness." This occurs when the Lord's word offends those who hear it and there is no desire for reconciliation with Him. Jeremiah outlines this scenario in 6:10 when he writes, "To whom can I speak and give warning? Who will listen to me? Their ears are closed so they cannot hear. The word of the Lord is offensive to them; they find no pleasure in it." They lack humility when they choose not to listen to the God of the Universe or heed his call for repairing relationships. In 44:10, it says, "To this day they have not humbled themselves or shown reverence, nor have they followed my law and the decrees I set before you and your ancestors" to describe their lack of reverence for who He is and continues to be. And yet there are others who believe themselves to be coy, who pretend to repent, but there is no wool being pulled over the Lord's eyes.

When sin has physical consequences, people often cry out to the Lord to stop it. As seen in 3:4-5, it can sound something like, "Have you not just called to me: 'My Father, my friend from my youth, will you always be angry? Will your wrath continue forever?' This is how you talk, but you do all the evil you can." The Israelites want God to end their suffering, but they would rather not repent; they just want their pain to stop. The calls for God's mercy are only an attempt at manipulating God to their own will. The Lord, seeing through the facade of self-interest, declares, "Despite all this, her unfaithful sister Judah did not return to me with all her heart, but only in pretense," in 3:10. The Lord can see our hearts and knows when our repentance is true or if it is a frail attempt to bend Him to our will.

Modern society often encourages us to "follow our hearts," but those who follow God directly discourage this type of mentality. Because when we follow our hearts and desires, it leads to situations where we only repent for selfish reasons and in pretense instead of a genuine rendering of our hearts before an all-merciful God to restore what was broken. Jeremiah points out the deception of our flesh in 7:24 when he says, "But they did not listen or pay attention; instead, they followed the stubborn inclinations of their evil hearts. They went backward and not forward." The irony in our selfish desire to only follow our hearts and wills is that when the Lord is asking us to return to Him, it is actually for our benefit.

Chapter 5, verse 25, says, "Your wrongdoings have kept these away; your sins have deprived you of good." Our lack of trust in what God says is good, righteous, and pure leads us to believe that what we have determined to be right, trustworthy, and helpful is greater than what He says. Moses in Deuteronomy 5:33 says, "Walk in obedience to all that the Lord your God has commanded you, so that you may live and prosper and prolong your days in the land that you will possess." He says in Deuteronomy to obey God so that it may go well with you. This is not the prosperity gospel!

Following God's commands is practical, and they are given for a reason. He may not always be quick to show us why something is wise; sometimes He asks us to do things the way He asks us to and to trust Him that it is what is best for us. When He asks us to do things His way and submit to Him in those moments, it is always for our good. When we have unrepentant sin and continue doing wrong, it keeps us from good. All of His commandments, even going back to the Ten Commandments, are to help us protect the relationships in our lives.

The first four commandments revolve around protecting our relationship with God Himself. These commandments include not having any other gods, not worshiping an image or false idol of anything in creation, refraining from misusing His name, and trusting Him to provide by taking a sabbath. All of those commands are to protect your relationship with Him. If you do any of those things, it breaks the relationship with Him and creates distance. The last six commandments give practical ways to not break relationships with others. Honoring your mother and father, not murdering people, not committing adultery, not stealing, lying, or coveting— these are all practical ways of keeping your relationships with other people intact. Engaging in any of those actions will undoubtedly damage your relationship with God and others. Therefore, when the Lord asks you to follow His ways, it's not because He's a cruel dictator who simply wants you to adhere to a set of rules. He is instructing you how to live a life that has healthy and meaningful relationships.

Outside of the 10 commandments, there are all types of rules and regulations that litter the Pentateuch. One might argue that they are quite strict and difficult to follow. But when you see that the Lord gave them these instructions out of love, it changes perspective. A positive example is how strict and detailed God was when giving the Israelites instructions for cleansing their bodies at multiple intervals throughout the day. We know now with modern science that germs, infections, and general uncleanliness can lead to sickness and death. But the Israelites didn't have that knowledge. The Lord told them to wash their hands and purify themselves before eating. As we can see thousands of years later, God was having them purify themselves for their protection but didn't go into detail about why He was telling them to do that in the moment. It required that they trust Him and that His regulations and rules were for their good. However, when we rebel against God and believe our ways are superior, our actions not only prevent us from doing good, but they can also severely harm us.

Changing our perspective of God from overbearing parent to loving and caring Father helps us see any resistance to repentance and reconciliation as foolishness. Unrepentance affects you and your health, and it also saddens the Lord. In 4:18-21, Jeremiah outlines the Lord's heart when we are stiff-necked by saying, "Your conduct and actions have brought this fate on you. The consequence is your punishment. How bitter it is! How it pierces the heart!" Oh, my anguish, my anguish! I writhe in pain. Oh, the agony of my heart! My heart pounds within me; I cannot keep silent. For I have heard the sound of the trumpet; I have heard the battle cry. Disaster follows disaster; the whole land lies in ruins. My tents vanish in an instant, along with my shelter. How long must I see the battle standard and hear the sound of the trumpet?" It pains Him when He sees us in pain, as seen in Jeremiah 8:21, which states, "Since my people are crushed, I am crushed; I mourn, and horror grips me." This is why the Lord never stops pursuing us.

God desires to be in relationship with us so much that he empathetically experiences our pain, even when it comes because of our sin. However, we repeatedly witness God's love for us through His unwavering pursuit of the Israelites. We see an example of such love in 7:13 when it says, "While you were doing all these things, declares the Lord, I spoke to you again and again, but you did not listen; I called you, but you did not answer." He is constantly drawing us back into a relationship with Him. The book of Hosea outlines the lengths to which He'll go out of love for us, and Jeremiah describes it perfectly in 31:3-6 when he says, "The Lord appeared to us in the past, saying, 'I have loved you with an everlasting love; I have drawn you with unfailing kindness. I will build you up again, and you, Virgin Israel, will be rebuilt. Again, you will take up your timbrels and go out to dance with the joyful. Again, you will plant vineyards on the hills of Samaria; the farmers will plant them and enjoy their fruit. There will be a day when watchmen cry out on the hills of

Ephraim, 'Come, let us go up to Zion, to the Lord our God.'" His desire is always for us to return to Him, to rebuild ourselves, and that "it may go well with us."

What does genuine repentance look like? It is paramount that we acknowledge our sin. Jeremiah provides a clear example of this in Jeremiah 14:20, where he speaks on behalf of the Israelites, "We acknowledge our wickedness, Lord, and the guilt of our ancestors; we have indeed sinned against you." Acknowledge sin, apologize, and turn the opposite way, living and acting in a way that contrasts with your previous state of mind and heart space. God speaks through Jeremiah, demonstrating His yearning for us and His immense compassion when we genuinely repent in 31:18-20. "Restore me, and I will return, because you are the Lord my God. After straying, I repented; upon understanding, I slapped my breast. I was ashamed because I bore the disgrace of my youth. Is not Ephraim my dear son, the child in whom I delight? Though I often speak against him, I still remember him. Therefore, my heart yearns for him; I have great compassion for him," declares the Lord."

God makes the following promises in 33:6-9 for those who are open-minded, quick to repent, and have a heart for reconciliation with Him: "Nevertheless, I will bring health and healing to it; I will heal my people and will let them enjoy abundant peace and security. I will bring Judah and Israel back from captivity, and I will rebuild them as they were before. I will cleanse them from all the sins they have committed against me and forgive all their rebellions against me. Then this city will make me famous, happy, and respected by all the nations that hear of my good deeds for it, and they will be amazed and afraid of the great peace and prosperity I bring."

God's heart is simple in this matter. His desire is for us to obey Him, not just for His benefit, but for ours. When we commit sin, we should recognize it, express regret, and move away from it. When we do this, we walk in the ways He has set out for us. Simply put, in 7:23, "Obey me, and I will be your God, and you will be my people. Walk in obedience to all I command you, that it may go well with you."

Questions to Ponder:

What is the modern meaning of being called "stiff-necked," and why is it a bad thing?

_____

_____

_____

_____

_____

_____

_____

_____

What does God ask of us when we sin, intentionally or not? What is His ultimate desire for us?

_____
_____
_____
_____
_____
_____
_____
_____

Why is unrepentance so offensive to God? What does it say about our hearts when we act this way?

_____
_____
_____
_____
_____
_____
_____
_____

What are markers of "true" repentance? Why is it impossible for us to fake it?

_____
_____
_____
_____

_____

_____

_____

_____

What might be the origins of our less genuine attempts at repentance?

_____

_____

_____

_____

_____

_____

_____

_____

Why is following God's commands practical?

_____

_____

_____

_____

_____

_____

_____

_____

What does God experience when we are unrepentant?

_____

_____

_____

_____

_____

_____

_____

_____

What does God promise those who are truly repentant, and what does that provide us?

_____

_____

_____

_____

_____

_____

_____

_____

Deceit & Intentional Disobedience

The depravity of man is a topic that has been explored en masse throughout human history. Whether through modern depictions in movies or by studying history, the Earth post-fall has consistently been mired in the depths of where man's sin will take them. Looking at the historical account of Moses in Exodus 32, we see that God wanted to destroy the Israelites, but Moses was able to advocate on their behalf, preventing His wrath from being poured onto them. The reason God felt the need to do that is, unfortunately, still pervasive among humankind today. Part of what Jeremiah is calling the Israelites out of is a life of unrestrained sin without repentance. This phenomenon is due to the New Testament's demonstration that God eventually relinquishes people to their wicked desires. Paul says in Romans 1:24-25, "Therefore God gave them over in the sinful desires of their hearts to sexual impurity for the degrading of their bodies with one another. They traded the truth about God for falsehoods and chose to worship and serve created things instead of the eternally praised Creator. Amen."

In the time that Jeremiah is prophesying to Israel, he describes them in 5:27-28: "Like cages full of birds, their houses are full of deceit; they have become rich and powerful and have grown fat and sleek. Their evil deeds have no limit; they do not seek justice. They do not promote the case of the fatherless; they do not defend the just cause of the poor." Note that he lists the consequences of living this way. 'Deceitful,' 'limitless evil,' 'neglecting justice,' 'not helping the orphan,' and 'ignoring a just cause because it comes from the poor.' The actions, or lack thereof, are examples of what happens when you pursue your desires without any restraint.

We all experience the temptation to lead a life that solely caters to our desires. The idea of "living our truth" or "following our hearts" may seem appealing, but it's important to understand that if everyone followed this path, it could potentially conflict with others around you. Eventually, if someone pursues their passions, it could hinder you from pursuing yours. In such a situation, how do you decide who deserves to have their way? Whose truth is more important? Why do they get to live their truth, but you can't live yours? This way of thinking is juvenile and short-sighted. And yet, even though this way of living is not logically coherent, our world continues to push it as the "only way to live" that is acceptable. However, this changes when you express a differing opinion.

Plainly put, Jeremiah 17:9 says, "The heart is deceitful above all things and beyond cure. Who can understand it?" Jeremiah 8:5-6 poses the question, "Why have these people turned away?" Why does Jerusalem always turn away? They cling to deceit; they refuse to return. I have listened attentively, but they do not say what is right. None of them repents of their wickedness, saying, "What have I done?" Each pursues their path, akin to a horse galloping into battle." Living for yourself and pursuing every whim and fancy comes at the expense of others around you. This is especially true for the vulnerable around you, who usually end up paying the price.

This way of thinking results in an egocentric pride that God fundamentally detests. Embracing a self-centered thought nucleus inevitably leads to the belief that nothing you do is 'wrong.' Jeremiah delves into this paradigm when he observes God's opposition, stating in 2:35b, "You claim to be innocent; God is not angry with me." However, God will judge you because you assert that you have not committed any sins." The ultimate version of pride is when one tries to tell the Creator of the universe that they are without fault or sin. What kind of delusion makes someone tell the omniscient, omnipotent, and timeless Lord of Lords that they are sinless? And yet Jeremiah describes the Israelites as those who "cling" to their deceit in 8:5.

Jeremiah says in 6:13, "From the least to the greatest, all are greedy for gain; prophets and priests alike, all practice deceit." This principle is further emphasized in Jeremiah's statement in 8:10, which states, "Therefore I will give their wives to other men and their fields to new owners." From the least to the greatest, all are greedy for gain; prophets and priests alike, all practice deceit." Even those that would be described as "righteous" and had titles like prophets and priests—the community Jeremiah was addressing— were all greedy for gain, practiced deceit, and had no shame. The Lord deeply grieves this posture of heart and mindset, especially among those He would call 'His people,' and will correct it.

Jeremiah dictates direct words from the Lord in 49:16 when He says, "The terror you inspire and the pride of your heart have deceived you, you who live in the clefts of the rocks, who occupy the heights of the hill. Though you build your nest as high as the eagle's, from there I will bring you down," declares the Lord." Proverbs 16:18 asserts that pride precedes destruction and an arrogant spirit precedes a fall. Pride is the antithesis of God. It is what caused Lucifer to fall, and we fall prey to the same thought processes that lead us to believe that we do not need God because of our strength, thoughts, ideas, and direction. When we live for ourselves instead of God, we may face natural consequences, but God may also correct us. In 2:19, God explains this dichotomy: "Your wickedness will punish you; your backsliding will rebuke you. The Lord Almighty says, "Think about how evil and bitter it is for you to forsake me, the Lord your God."

It is easy to get wrapped up in the ecosystem of self, especially in Western culture. Who you surround yourself with plays a giant part in who you become. You become like those you spend the most time with, and bad choices can have dire effects. In 9:4-6, Jeremiah warns of the Israelite community's shared rebellious behavior. "Beware of your friends; do not trust anyone in your clan. For every one of them is a deceiver, and every friend a slanderer. A friend deceives another, and no one speaks the truth. They have taught their tongues to lie; they weary themselves with sinning. You live amid deception; in their deceit, they refuse to acknowledge me," declares the Lord." But how do we combat this pervasive idea, which our modern culture encourages everywhere?

This requires radical confession and repentance. This type of lifestyle is difficult but immensely helpful in combating the pull of self-absorption and pride. It begins with acknowledging our sin truthfully and holistically. Jeremiah 3:13 gives us an example when he says, "Only acknowledge your guilt—you have rebelled against the Lord your God, you have scattered your favors to foreign gods under every spreading tree, and you have not obeyed me', declares the Lord." Call your sin what it is, rebellion against God and His ways. Does that sound severe? Good. This is the truth. All sins, even the seemingly insignificant ones you may think no one cares about, ultimately lead to death. If all you ever did was commit that one 'small' sin your whole life and you didn't repent or have a relationship with God, that 'small' sin would send you to eternal separation from Him. Our only course of action is to confess, repent, walk the opposite direction, and seek His will and direction for our lives.

That may sound simple, but the Israelites had trouble with this as well. It wasn't bad enough that they had pride that got in the way of developing a relationship with God; they also intentionally disobeyed Him after He gave them clear direction. The account of Johanan's band of Israelites in Jeremiah is a perfect example of the consequences of this pride. The chapters leading up to 42 help illustrate how Johanan came to take this position of leadership and provide a picture of what is happening.

In Jeremiah 37, Jeremiah is thrown in prison for the messages he was communicating on behalf of God. Later in chapter 39 when King Nebuchadnezzar took over

Jerusalem, Jeremiah was freed by the commander of the Imperial Guard in chapter 40. At that point, most of the Israelites were in captivity except for the remaining remnant who had settled in Mizpah. Gedaliah, who was the governor of that remnant was warned by Johanan (an army officer) that Baalis the King of the Ammonites sent Ishmael to kill him. Gedaliah doesn't believe Johanan and pays the ultimate price when he is assassinated by him. At this point, Ishmael takes all the Israelites who were living in Mizpah captive, removing them from their homes. Johanan as a military officer, pursues Ishmael and his captives with a small band of men, confronts them and Ishmael and his eight buddies flee. Johanan and his companions lead the captives but are afraid to bring them back to Mizpah because the governor who had been assigned by Babylon to lead this remnant of Israel was killed. He was stuck and didn't know what to do, which is where Jeremiah comes in.

Johanan didn't know where to take the people or what he should do. He seeks Jeremiah, and they have this exchange in 42:3-6: "Pray that the Lord your God will tell us where we should go and what we should do." "I have heard you," replied Jeremiah the prophet. "I will certainly pray to the Lord your God as you have requested; I will tell you everything the Lord says and will keep nothing back from you." Then they said to Jeremiah, "May the Lord be a true and faithful witness against us if we do not act by everything the Lord, your God, sends you to tell us. We will obey the Lord our God, to whom we send you, for our good." The words are bold and appear to be well-intentioned. They respond exactly how the Lord would hope they would. They are similar to Shadrach, Meshach, and Abednego in Daniel 3:16–18 when they are facing the fiery furnace. "They replied to him, King Nebuchadnezzar, we do not need to defend ourselves before you in this matter. If we are thrown into the blazing furnace, the God we serve can deliver us from it, and he will deliver us from Your Majesty's hand. But even if He doesn't, we want you to know, Your Majesty, that we will not serve your gods or worship the image of gold you have set up." These are the right things to say, but you better be ready to back those words up.

If you ask the Lord for guidance on where you should go and what you should do, you'd better be prepared to follow through on your end. If you ask Him what His will is, He makes it clear, and you choose to disobey, it would have been better for you if you had not asked at all. Jeremiah makes clear, after spending ten days seeking the Lord in this matter, that the Israelites should stay in the land. He says in 42:10-12, "'If you stay in this land, I will build you up and not tear you down; I will plant you and not uproot you, for I have relented concerning the disaster I have inflicted on you. Do not be afraid of the king of Babylon, whom you now fear. The Lord says, "Don't fear him; I will save you." I will show you compassion, and he will have compassion on you and restore you to your land." In this rare case, God makes Himself explicitly clear that He will be with them and restore them if they trust Him.

He then tells them what the consequence will be if they don't trust him in 42:13-18 when He says, ""However, if you say, 'We will not stay in this land,' and so disobey the Lord your God, and if you say, 'No, we will go and live in Egypt, where we will not see war or hear the trumpet or be hungry for bread,' then hear the word of the Lord, you remnant of Judah. This is what the Lord Almighty, the God of Israel, says: 'If you are determined to go to Egypt and you do go to settle there, then the sword you fear will overtake you there, and the famine you dread will follow you into Egypt, and there you will die. Indeed, all who are determined to go to Egypt to settle there will die by the sword, famine, and plague; not one of them will survive or escape the disaster I will bring on them.' This is what the Lord Almighty, the God of Israel, says: 'As my anger and wrath have been poured out on those who lived in Jerusalem, so will my wrath be poured out on you when you go to Egypt. You will be a curse and an object of horror, a curse and an object of reproach; you will never see this place again.'" God is asking them to trust Him and to stay in the land they were in under Nebuchadnezzar's rule, while the Israelites want to flee back to Egypt, which is something the Israelites struggled with for generations.

Jeremiah attempts to warn them, knowing that they would likely not listen in 42:19-22 when he tells them, ""Remnant of Judah, the Lord has told you, 'Do not go to Egypt.' Be sure of this: I warn you today that you made a fatal mistake when you sent me to the Lord your God and said, 'Pray to the Lord our God for us; tell us everything he says and we will do it.' I have told you today, but you still have not obeyed the Lord your God in all he sent me to tell you. So now, be sure of this: You will die by the sword, famine, and plague in the place where you want to go to settle." Sure enough, their response was flooded with pride, ego, and self-righteousness when they said in 43:2-3, "Azariah son of Hoshaiah and Johanan's son of Kareah and all the arrogant men said to Jeremiah, 'You are lying! The Lord our God has not sent you to say, 'You must not go to Egypt to settle there.' But Baruch, son of Neriah, is inciting you against us to hand us over to the Babylonians, so they may kill us or carry us into exile to Babylon."

Johanan and his men didn't like the answer when they asked the Lord, and in their arrogance and paranoia, they intentionally disobeyed God. 43:4-5 says, "So Johanan, son of Kareah, and all the army officers and all the people disobeyed the Lord's command to stay in the land of Judah." Johanan, son of Kareah, and the army officers gathered all the remnants of Judah that had returned from their scattered nations." Jeremiah expresses the truth starkly when he informs them that they had indeed made a "fatal mistake." They made a request to the Lord for guidance, but had no intention of following the Lord's commands if it didn't fit their own desired outcomes.

Despite Jeremiah's rebuke, they persist in their sinful ways, disobeying God and flaunting it to Jeremiah and the Lord. They display their bold and blatant disobedient hearts in 44:16-18 when they declare, "We will not listen to the message you have spoken to us in the name of the Lord! We will certainly do everything we said we would: we will burn incense to the Queen of Heaven and pour out drink offerings to her just as we, our ancestors, our kings, and our officials did in the towns of Judah and the streets of Jerusalem. At that time, we had plenty of food, were well off, and suffered no harm. But ever since we stopped burning incense to the Queen of Heaven and pouring out drink offerings to her, we have had nothing and have been perishing by sword and famine."

It is easy to console ourselves that if the Lord were clear in His direction for us, we would obey without hesitation. Yet, we see example after example in the book of Jeremiah where the Lord is abundantly clear with the Israelites, and they blatantly disobey. The ways of this world are alluring for a reason. A life fully dominated by our selfishness, controlled by our desires, and revolving around our whims and fancies without any regard for others is a tempting worldview. But what we know from the Scriptures and from our relationship with Him is that what the Lord has for us is so much greater than anything that type of life could produce. Our ideas will always fall short of the grand narrative that God is weaving through human history. Isaiah says it best in Isaiah 55:8-9, "For my thoughts are not your thoughts, neither are your ways my ways," declares the Lord. "As the heavens are higher than the earth, so are my ways higher than your ways and my thoughts than your thoughts."

Willfully living in an ego-centric mentality with no regard for God's will for your life is a surefire way to destruction. If we live for ourselves and our advancement, we have nothing. Praying for His leading in your life is a way to find peace in chaos, but be prepared to obey it, regardless of where that prayer leads you. Not knowing His will is better than knowing it and disobeying. The hubris of western culture permeates everything about our society, but God calls us to live a different way. His way.

Questions to Ponder:

What specific characteristics of the Israelites did Jeremiah call out that God wanted them to repent for?

_____

_____

_____

_____

_____

_____

_____

_____

Explain why the concepts of "living your truth" or "following your heart" are logically incoherent.

_____

_____

_____

_____

_____

_____

_____

_____

What is the ultimate form of pride'?

_____

_____

_____

_____

_____

_____

_____

_____

Explain how followers of God are just as prone to fall prey to their ego as the world is.

_____

_____

_____

_____

_____

_____

_____

Explain why pride is the 'antitheses' of God.

_____

_____

_____

_____

_____

_____

_____

What was Johanan's "fatal mistake' while leading the remnant of Israel?

_____

_____

_____

_____

_____

_____

_____

_____

_____

_____

_____

Oppression

The Old and New Testaments say that those who claim to be with God must care for the helpless. God demands that His people have compassion and act on behalf of the foreigner, orphan, widow, and innocent. Not only are His people called to help these people groups, but He also makes specific mention that His people are not to oppress them.

'Oppression' is a word that is thrown around too loosely in our modern context and has lost some of its depth and true meaning. Going with it are words like 'genocide,' 'abuse,' or 'colonization.' These words have been co-opted by other movements and used flippantly to describe world events when those things aren't actually happening. However, the people using them know that those words cause physical and visceral responses in most cases, so they use them to hyperbolize their points of view. Whether you are the one using these words out of their proper context or you hear them, most people, when they realize that isn't the reality of a situation, tend to tune out the rest of what is being said. The reason why oppression is brought up in the book of Jeremiah is because Israel was swallowed up by it. As we see in 6:6, God speaks directly to their wickedness: "This is what the Lord Almighty says: 'Cut down the trees and build siege ramps against Jerusalem. We must punish this city for its oppression.'"

There are many definitions of what oppression may or may not have looked like, but there are specific verses that describe the kind of oppression that Israel was participating in that God abhors. In 7:3-8 it says, "This is what the Lord Almighty, the God of Israel, says: 'Reform your ways and your actions, and I will let you live in this place. Do not trust in deceptive words" and say, "This is the temple of the Lord, the temple of the Lord, the temple of the Lord!" If you really change your ways and your actions and deal with each other justly, if you do not oppress the foreigner, the fatherless, or the widow and do not shed innocent blood in this place, and if you do not follow other gods to your harm, then I will let you live in this place, in the land I gave your ancestors forever and ever. But look, you are trusting in deceptive words that are worthless."

Sadly, both political parties in the United States have politicized and radicalized care and compassion for these marginalized groups. Jesus specifically calls followers of Him to serve these same people groups in Matthew 25 when He says we should care for the "least of these." And as we see in Jeremiah, God is rebuking the nation of Israel for how they are acting unjustly by oppressing the foreigner, the orphan, the widow, and the innocent. So, what does it mean to 'oppress' someone? In the English language, it means "prolonged cruelty or unjust treatment or control." It is interesting to see that Jeremiah linked oppression with the same thing that the Oxford Dictionary does: a lack of justice.

It is easy to overlook these vulnerable people groups. All of them require attention and care from society. They all need compassion, empathy, and resources to continue living. These people are often mistreated because they can be with very little recourse. This is why the Lord, through Jeremiah, establishes that the initial step towards aiding these individuals is to treat them justly. It doesn't mention their physical needs first, or why they need help in the first place. He says that Israel should be known for how it treats its people justly. John 13:35 gives a New Testament example of what such behavior looks like when he says, "By this all people will know that you are my disciples, if you have love for one another." Instead, these people are abused, mistreated, and used as political pawns to achieve power and control. These systems enrich those who set them up, which falls into the category of 'toxic charity,' only provide short-term help, and eventually cause people to end up in more situations where they need further assistance.

God's heart is for the lost, broken, and needy. As He shows through Jeremiah, He takes it very seriously if His people are uncaring toward these people groups. To the point where He is willing to tear down everything to get that point across. In 45:2-5 in his message to Baruch, he says, "When Baruch son of Neriah wrote on a scroll the words Jeremiah the prophet dictated in the fourth year of Jehoiakim son of Josiah king of Judah, Jeremiah said this to Baruch: 'This is what the Lord, the God of Israel, says to you, Baruch: You said, 'Woe to me! The Lord has added sorrow to my pain; I am worn out with groaning and find no rest.' But the Lord has told me to say to you, 'This is what the Lord says: I will overthrow what I have built and uproot what I have planted throughout the earth. Should you then seek great things for yourself? Do not seek them. For I will bring disaster on all people, declares the Lord, but wherever you go I will let you escape with your life.'"

If people claim to love God and yet oppress these groups, they are lying. John conveys a similar message in 1 John 4:19-21 of the New Testament: "We love because

He first loved us. Anyone who professes to love God but harbors hatred toward their brother or sister is dishonest. For whoever does not love their brother and sister, whom they have seen, cannot love God, whom they have not seen. And He has given us this command: Anyone who loves God must also love their brother and sister." Going back to Jeremiah 7:3-8, it said, "...Do not trust in deceptive words and say, 'This is the temple of the Lord, the temple of the Lord, the temple of the Lord!" People often claim to be followers of the Lord, yet condemn those they should show compassion to. This is a genuine interpretation of "taking the Lord's name in vain."

In modern times it is not uncommon to hear people saying that they walked away from the Lord because of the actions of those in the Church. They attribute characteristics to God that are false when those who claim His name inflict harm upon them. When we claim to be followers of Christ and declare it outwardly, we are held to a higher standard. Just like the Israelites were held to a higher standard because neighboring countries knew that they were God's chosen people. Which is why God takes those who are acting on His behalf very seriously

In Jeremiah 21:12 we see the truth when it says, "This is what the Lord says to you, house of David: 'Administer justice every morning; rescue from the hand of the oppressor the one who has been robbed, or my wrath will break out and burn like fire because of the evil you have done—burn with no one to quench it." The heart of God is to love all people, period. This includes those who are marginalized, oppressed, persecuted, and abandoned. We know this because we see God do this on behalf of the Israelites when they fit one of those descriptions. In 50:33-34, it describes how He views them in their season of exile: "This is what the Lord Almighty says: 'The people of Israel are oppressed, and the people of Judah as well. All their captors hold them fast, refusing to let them go. Yet their Redeemer is strong; the Lord Almighty is his name. He will vigorously defend their cause so that he may bring rest to their land but unrest to those who live in Babylon."

Living in God's truth, obeying His word, and carrying out His will is always going to revolve around loving all people and treating them justly. Always. By treating them with restoration, reconciliation, and justice, we should embody God's heart. In 30:3 it demonstrates God's heart when it says, "The days are coming,' declares the Lord, "when I will bring my people Israel and Judah back from captivity and restore them to the land I gave their ancestors to possess,' says the Lord." Oppressing the vulnerable is wicked. What a political party says or how a foreign policy scares you is irrelevant. God tells the Israelites the benefits of caring for the most vulnerable. In Jeremiah 29:7, it says, "Also, seek the peace and prosperity of the city to which I have carried you into exile. Pray to the Lord for it, because if it prospers, you too will prosper."

This isn't the prosperity gospel; this is fruit. When we sow seeds of compassion, empathy, and care for those who are considered the "least of these," it will be like we have taken care of Christ Himself. Those who are oppressed need our time, resources, and attention. We must seek justice for them, do everything within our power to free them from oppression, and refrain from placing them in those situations to begin with.

Questions to Ponder:

Why has the word 'oppression' lost some of its meaning in our current vernacular?

_____
_____
_____
_____
_____
_____
_____
_____

Who are the groups that God lists as those Israel was oppressing? Why are they particularly vulnerable?

_____
_____

_____

_____

_____

_____

_____

_____

In general, how do we use marginalized people as political pawns?

_____

_____

_____

_____

_____

_____

_____

_____

What does it mean to 'take the Lord's name in vain' in a broader context than just saying His name when we stub our toe?

_____

_____

_____

_____

_____

_____

_____

_____

Why is claiming you are doing something on behalf of God' dangerous, and why must you be right if that is the case?

_____

_____

_____

_____

_____

_____

_____

How can Christians better serve marginalized people TODAY?

_____

_____

_____

_____

_____

_____

_____

_____

True Godly Character/Righteousness

The Bible is filled with guidance and illustrations of what it means to be righteous in the Lord's eyes. There are numerous examples of once-faithful individuals abandoning Him in favor of idols. He responds to the dire events and situations that cause His people to cry out in agony for His salvation. They or their kin turn their backs on Him yet again. But this unfaithfulness isn't just a belief issue; their actions directly contradict what He asks of His people. God makes it clear throughout Scripture that believing in Him requires confession, repentance, and ardently following Him with action. Jeremiah is no different.

In Jeremiah 35, the Lord shows the Israelites the Rechabites as an example. He is perplexed that this clan of people obediently follows directives from their ancestor and holds to them without wavering. And yet, the people of Israel hear direct words from the Lord who saved their people from Egypt, performing many miracles along the way, and they refuse to obey Him from generation to generation.

'Go to the Rechabite family and invite them to one of the side rooms of the house of the Lord and give them wine to drink,' said the Lord to Jeremiah during Jehoiakim's reign." So, I went to get Jaazaniah, son of Jeremiah, the son of Habazziniah, and his brothers and all his sons—the whole family of the Rechabites. I brought them into the Lord's house—into the room of Hanan, son of Igdaliah, the man of God. It was next to the officials' room, above Maaseiah, Shallum's son, the doorkeeper. Then I set bowls full of wine and some cups before the Rechabites and said to them, "Drink some wine." But they replied, "We do not drink wine because our forefather Jehonadab, son of Rechab, gave us this command: 'Neither you nor your descendants must ever drink spirits. Furthermore, you must never build houses, sow seed, or plant vineyards; you must never have any of these things but must always live in tents. Then you will live a long time in the land where you are nomads.' We have obeyed everything our forefather Jehonadab, son of Rechab, commanded us. Neither we nor our wives nor our sons and daughters have ever drunk wine or built houses to live in or had vineyards, fields, or crops. We have lived in tents and have fully obeyed everything our forefather Jehonadab commanded us. But when Nebuchadnezzar, king of Babylon, invaded this land, we said, 'Come, we must go to Jerusalem to escape the Babylonian and Aramean armies.' So, we have remained in Jerusalem." Then the word of the Lord came to Jeremiah, saying, "This is what the Lord Almighty, the God of Israel, says: Go and tell the people of Judah and those living in Jerusalem, 'Will you not learn a lesson and obey my words?' declares the Lord. Jehonadab, son of Rechab, ordered his descendants not to drink wine, and this command has been kept. To this day, they do not drink wine because they obey their forefather's command. I have repeatedly spoken to you, but you have not obeyed me. Again and again, I sent all my servants, the prophets, to you. They said, "Each of you must turn from your wicked ways and reform your actions; do not follow other gods to serve them. Then you will live in the land I have given to you and your ancestors." But you have not paid attention or listened to me. The descendants of Jehonadab, son of Rechab, have carried out the command their forefather gave them, but these people have not obeyed me.' "Therefore, this is what the Lord God Almighty, the God of Israel, says: 'Listen! I am going to bring on Judah and on everyone living in Jerusalem every disaster I pronounced against them. I spoke to them, but they did not listen; I called to them, but they did not answer.'" Then Jeremiah said to the family of the Rechabites, "This is what the Lord Almighty, the God of Israel, says: 'You have obeyed the command of your forefather Jehonadab and have followed all his instructions and have done everything he ordered.' Therefore, this is what the Lord Almighty, the God of Israel, says: "Jehonadab, son of Rechab, will never fail to have a descendant to serve me.'"

The Rechabites had no reason to obey their ancestors' orders except to respect them and their customs. God uses them as an example to the Israelites because it should be easier for them to follow His ways than for this clan to follow theirs. They are prohibited from drinking wine, building homes, sowing a field, and providing for themselves, all of which are difficult directives. Yet, they faithfully followed them. God is making plain that our actions in light of what He calls us to do matter, and our words by themselves yield nothing.

Our character can't just be in what we "say"; it is in what we "do." The Lord sees right through the duplicitous nature of our hearts, just like He did with the Israelites. In 5:1-2, he calls it out, saying, "Go up and down the streets of Jerusalem, look around and consider, and search through her squares." If you can find but one person who deals honestly and seeks the truth, I will forgive this city. Although they say, 'As surely as the Lord lives,' still they are swearing falsely." Even though they swear by His name, they are dishonest and untrustworthy. They use His name in vain, pretending to be righteous while behaving deceitfully.

Numerous passages in the New Testament address the same issue. One of which is found in James 2:14, where the author asks, "What good is it, my brothers and sisters, if someone claims to have faith but has no deeds?" Often, we use this passage to explore the idea of salvation, but it reflects the mindset that the Lord challenges in Jeremiah. If you have true faith in the Lord, your actions will demonstrate that. Your actions cannot save you, but they reveal your true allegiance. Our actions reveal our character. Particularly during challenging times, our true beliefs become evident. A verse in James that discusses our character is in 4:17, where he says, "If anyone, then, knows the good they ought to do and doesn't do it, it is sin for them." Sometimes we will intellectually know the right thing to do or even by directly led by God to act and yet we don't obey. These areas of our lives tend to lead to mental gymnastics that can help us cope with our disobedience, but that doesn't make it any less sinful. Therefore, we must pay attention if someone confronts or accuses us of a character flaw. Jeremiah puts it bluntly in 13:15 when he says, "Hear and pay attention; do not be arrogant, for the Lord has spoken." To become who God created us to be, we must begin with a heart posture of humility and coachability, which is not often found or celebrated in our modern age. But when we do, the result is staggering.

Jeremiah spends most of the book he wrote and the time he spent as a prophet calling the Israelites to repentance and speaking harsh truths. But he also outlines the beauty of how following God within a righteous context can truly bless your life too. Our interactions with God stop being a 'mandated chore' and turn into our most coveted time of the day. 15:16 says, "When your words came, I ate them; they were my joy and my heart's delight, for I bear your name, Lord God Almighty." Hearing from the Lord no longer comes with fear of consequence but instead a boon of relationship that remains with us as we navigate life. Our prayer life ceases to be a pre-meal obligation and turns into a daylong conversation that penetrates all aspects of our lives. There is security and peace that comes from living in full submission to the Lord and His will. We can trust that the Lord will direct our steps and fulfill His promises. 10:23 says, "Lord, I know that people's lives are not their own; it is not for them to direct their steps."

Our lives begin to take an eternal shape that will affect not just ourselves but all around us. An unwavering character bolsters us, enabling us to say and do things we never thought possible in various situations. The words He places on our tongues create an urgency where they must come out. Jeremiah illustrates this in 20:9 when he says, 'But if I say, 'I will not mention his word or speak anymore in his name,' his word is in my heart like a fire, a fire shut up in my bones. I am weary of holding it in; indeed, I cannot." Every interaction has eternal stakes; each morning you wake up is a new opportunity to take ground for the Kingdom, and there is a unique energy behind everything you do. We must handle this exciting new paradigm with wisdom.

Occasionally, we begin running faster than our current spiritual maturity can handle. Oftentimes in our exuberance of freedom, we extend ourselves further than our character is ready for. Jeremiah warns in 12:5, "If you have raced with men on foot and they have worn you out, how can you compete with horses?" If you stumble in safe country, how will you manage in the thickets by the Jordan?" But when He brings you back, it is always motivated by love, abundant grace, and guidance. His desire is for us to become one with Him. 32:38-39 says, "They will be my people, and I will be their God. I will give them unity of heart and action so they will always fear me, and all will go well for them and their children." In our human nature, we believe that we want choices. We desire to control our actions and words. However, as one begins to mature in their faith, they realize that placing any kind of trust in ourselves over the Lord is always a fruitless endeavor.

Jeremiah's most famous verse speaks to the Lord's character, but not in the ways that are often incorrectly used. People often adorn household signs, screensavers, and coffee mugs with Jeremiah 29:11, a motivational verse they find inspiring. Why wouldn't they? It's so positive! The issue is that the Lord is speaking to a specific group of Israelites who are coming out of seventy years of exile, not to all believers. In context, we can still glean encouraging truths from verses 29:10-14: "This is what the Lord says: 'When seventy years are completed for Babylon, I will come to you and fulfill my beneficial promise to bring you back to this place. For I know the plans I have for you,' declares the Lord, "plans to prosper you and not to harm you, plans to give you hope and a future. Then you will call on me and come and pray to me, and I will listen to you. You will seek me and find me when you search for me with all your heart. You will find me, declares the Lord, and I will bring you back from captivity. The Lord says, "I will gather you from all the nations and places where I have banished you and bring you back to the place from which I carried you into exile."

If someone says, "For I know the plans I have for you—plans to prosper you and not harm you, plans to give you hope and a future" and applies them prescriptively to their lives, what happens when negative experiences inevitably occur? Living in a broken, sinful world guarantees hardship. Jesus promises us too that when we follow Him, the world will hate us the same way they hated Him (John 15:18). People can begin to question God, themselves, their faith, or even worse, walk away from the Lord because they believe He let them down when He never promised us a life without difficulty. When we hold God to commitments He never made, that only hurts us. There is still so much that can be gleaned from the entirety of verses 10-14.

The Lord always fulfills His promises. Always. God will fulfill the promises He has given us, just as the Lord took the Israelites out of their seventy-year captivity and brought them prosperity, security, hope, and a future. Joshua repeats it twice: once after the Israelites conquered Canaan and again as they entered the Promised Land. In Joshua 21:45, he says, "Not one of all the Lord's good promises to the house of Israel failed; everyone was fulfilled," and in 23:14, he says, "Now I am about to go the way of all the earth. You are fully aware that the Lord, your God, has fulfilled all the good promises He gave you. Every promise has been fulfilled; not one has failed." This theme echoes throughout both the Old and the New Testament. God is who He says He is.

The central component of our character must come from a place of true belief that God is who He says He is. He will fulfill every promise He has ever made and bring to fruition the covenants He has established. Our hope comes from the core tenets of our faith, which is where our character springs from. If so, we can live by the spirit's fruit while awaiting what's next. We trust that living according to His blueprint is more beneficial for us than any alternative we could devise. We are only righteous because of what He did, not because of anything we do in return. When God the Father sees us, He sees Christ's sacrifice on the cross and His holiness. It is not anything we do that saves us for eternity. Belief, confession, repentance, and action are the key components. We can be confident that the sanctification process will take root when we follow Him with everything we have, keeping our hands open to His guidance, obeying, and enjoying a relationship with Him. He will continue to make us more and more like Him, growing in our character day to day, hour by hour, minute to minute.

Questions to Ponder:

What was the Lord trying to teach the Israelites from the example of the Rechabites?

_____

_____

_____

_____

_____

_____

_____

_____

What type of situations reveal our true character at that
current point?

_____

_____

_____

_____

_____

_____

_____

_____

Explain why our character can't just be in what we say.

_____

_____

_____

_____

_____

_____

_____

_____

_____

_____

_____

Is It Just?

Explain how full submission to God can reshape your life and perspective on your relationship with Him and all that comes with it.

_____

_____

_____

_____

_____

_____

_____

_____

Explain how accepting that "it's not up to you to direct your steps" brings freedom.

_____

_____

_____

_____

_____

_____

_____

_____

Why is it dangerous to take Jeremiah 29:11 out of context?

_____

_____

_____

_____

_____

_____

_____

_____

Why is it important to trust that God is who He says He is?

_____

_____

_____

_____

_____

_____

_____

How is true Godly character and righteousness formed in us?

_____

_____

_____

_____

_____

_____

_____

_____

_____

About
Kharis Publishing:

Kharis Publishing, an imprint of Kharis Media LLC, is a leading Christian and inspirational book publisher based in Aurora, Chicago metropolitan area, Illinois. Kharis' dual mission is to give voice to under-represented writers (including women and first-time authors) and equip orphans in developing countries with literacy tools. That is why, for each book sold, the publisher channels some of the proceeds into providing books and computers for orphanages in developing countries so that these kids may learn to read, dream, and grow. For a limited time, Kharis Publishing is accepting unsolicited queries for nonfiction (Christian, self-help, memoirs, business, health and wellness) from qualified leaders, professionals, pastors, and ministers. Learn more at:
 https://kharispublishing.com/

www.ingramcontent.com/pod-product-compliance
Lightning Source LLC
LaVergne TN
LVHW051745080426
835511LV00018B/3233